NO STRUCTURE PLEASE:

A Poetic Liberation

Gioya Tuma-Waku
+
Chaise Angelo Tait

More information at www.perfectlyimperfectent.com

Cover illustration by Gioya Tuma-Waku.

ISBN: 978-1-7347659-0-8

First Edition: April 2020

Dedicated to X, without you, I'm not sure how long before I
would have gotten back into writing.
Thank you for the journey that started in 2018.
All the highs, lows and art paved the way for this.
And to my family, and friends, I truly appreciate all your love
and continued support.
Poetry is my therapy.
-Gioya Tuma-Waku

I want to dedicate this book to all the profound people in my life
who experienced this rollercoaster of colors with me. I hope this
book finds you all with love.
-Chaise Angelo Tait

FOREPLAY

We been side by side for months, yet we still don't speak
the same language,

I'm starting to grow a little anxious.

Ain't no growth in this cause we can't seem to find time
for patience,

It's like we speaking sign language,

And we keep our words short so we don't become
violated,

It's like an infinite cycle of being continuously dilated,

I feel woozy when I see you,

My mind loves to get caught in your web,

And now I'm in your bed,

Calm as shit cause you know what comes next,

The tossing and turning morphs into intimate sex.

I already got you,

I slipped you a kiss and your lips loved every dropful,

Time is of the essence I'm just taking my chances,

I put this image in my mind of you doing dirty dances.

You're on top of me whirling like your painting a beautiful
canvas.

You're the artist and I'm the paintbrush,

Draw me in your image and I'll frame it one day,

We'll look back and call it our little foreplay.

-C.A.T

RESENTMENT

I resent the girl who ruined you for me

I resent her because she had the best part of you

She had your joy and love

and for a little while it was enough

But when she was done

Instead of returning it to you

She threw it all away

Now you're here

And I'm here

And we're right but time isn't

I want to wrap you in my love

Turn your scars to beauty marks

Make you forget she broke your heart

Stare into my eyes so you see my soul

Let it wash away your tears

As my joy heals your heart

So you are forever by my side

But I can't be what you want

And you can't be what I want

And so here I stand

My soul crying for yours

My heart weeping for yours

My tears falling for your love

But it's not enough

And I'm not enough

So what is enough?

All you see is Black

All I see is white

So I resent her for taking our colour

And throwing it into the night

-G.TW

CHOICES

There is a life inside of me that yells please so softly.

Like a whisper through the trees,

I'm finding my voice,

To live the life of a legend or die trying to be one at my own discretion,

Or am I pressin'?

I'm finally being tested but I'm not stressin',

The waters of my deep soul that ripple when I create the perfect timbre,

For an imperfect ghetto boy,

Lord knows I had no toys,

Just thoughts,

An endless road of unpaved road,

I'm taking the backroads,

Lo and behold,

My story has been told.

-C.A.T

I don't belong here

I don't belong there

I don't belong anywhere

-G.TW

COLD NIGHTS

Time's ticking and I don't know where I'll fit in,

Maybe I hate this shit and want it to end.

Running doesn't do the trick,

Neither does hiding.

I've done that for almost 3 decades and you just become slimy.

All your empty thoughts transform into fear,

And just painting them won't make it stop being fear.

So what do I do when I feel that knot in my throat,

A bag of anxious thoughts, and time fading away on the clock?

I imagine my own universe and say I am God.

-C.A.T

I LOVE YOU

I love you

Dare I say it

I love you

More than the stars love the sky

More than that twinkle in your eye

I love you

Like every strand of growing hair

And through every moment of pain

I love you

Even through the thought of losing you

You've taken over my whole being

And so with that my whole existence

Just loves you

-G.TW

CRUSHING HARD

When I wake up,

The world is quiet,

The sun still sleeps,

And the moon is tired.

But you,

You never fade away,

I destroy fear when you walk by my side,

I wish I had treated you without fear,

But now you walk hand in hand with a boy at our local fair,

I wanted to win you a teddy bear.

I'm not crying,

These tears are just from the smoke that hasn't cleared.

I lock myself in my room,

Trying to cope with thoughts that lurk and loom,

I see your face on a blank canvas full of vibrant colors,

Wondering if that will ever be the face of another?

I'd walk for miles you never stopped following me,

I think it's because you're onto me.

Some call it a crush,

But I think it's just lust.

-C.A.T

I can only fight for this for as long as

You're willing to fight by my side

-G.TW

DODGE AVENGER

Mamma, how'd you do that shit?

You bought me clothes that made me feel fucking legit,

You told me to put books first so I went out and carved hieroglyphs,

You showed me black history and now my foundation is solid,

I search for hidden mysteries that are deeper than just cosmic.

Human intellect is not my logic,

I'll swallow that bitch whole with eternal imagination,

And false prophets think that's the situation,

Stop dodging and just center yourself,

Find what you need and avenge yourself.

-C.A.T

Sometimes confident, mostly lost

Always battling two opposing sides

I walk alone

A life of outside opinions with shallow insight

All I can be is true to me

While going against the tide

A life on my terms is worth all the fight

-G.TW

DON'T WAIT UP

Hey kid, don't wait up on anyone,

The time is now little one,

You spent the past month thinking about thinking,

Little did you know your ambition wasn't leaving,

So you tied it up and threw it outside,

Oh now you wanna know what's beyond the limit of the sky?

If ego will always try to control our minds?

Or will you change your mentality and stop being so blind,

Maybe then you won't have to waste your mind.

You can just go and fly because you believe inside.

So hey kid,

Don't wait up this time.

-C.A.T

Pure art exists in a place where chains are broken

-G.TW

NOT A BIBLE TYPE LOVE

Love is overwhelming and encompassing

Yes it's patient, yes it's kind

But it's not always easy

However when perfect souls align

As if by design

Love flows freely and it's divine

Unconditional it can be

Never failing it should be

But what happens when your heart's on fire

And the only one who can extinguish it

Is the same person who lit you up

It always protects, trusts, hopes, perseveres

It's like air, you can't feel it

But you know it's there

A spirit gently moving through

It's in every song, poem or movie

But what if it also feels

Like a sharp pain through your chest

As you struggle to grasp for air

Over and over the jabs come

Attacking the very core of you

Until you're weak and limp

Do you rely on it or move to self-preservation?

Love your family, love your friends

Love your partners in order to mend

But love yourself like no one else

Because you can light up your own heart

With what brings you joy

And it won't burn

Not even a little bit, not even at all

-G.TW

EDITED

It seems loving you has been a bit too much,

I can't stand to be around myself so my thoughts tend to depart.

I'm tryna attain some type of concentration,

So I won't feel like I'm in a concentration,

Campaigning for myself because I have energy for no one else.

I'm selfish as fuck but I promise you it's for good reason,

I never had anything of my own so now every season is a new reason.

I have no idea where to start,

I wish I had a big brother or a dad to tell me bro don't be a shark,

Take your blessings and create an art,

Fill the room with bodies that aren't chained to the iron,

But forged in the fire and made with deep desire,

Words I can't find begin to sprout from the roof of my mind,

But lack of resources got me thinking again about my crimes,

I made it past the system only to be addicted to passing the time,

Medicating because all I do is cry,

But I feel nothing so how am I alive,

I've tried,

But should I try more,

The only way to get through is to believe you are more,

I don't wanna hurt nobody but people need to hear my truth,

It could be the springboard for that one voice within a million.

Even if the title only resonates with you,

It can hold you, when you've lost you, and it's time to finally stand up,

You give yourself not nearly enough credit,

But deep inside you just wish you could leave out all the edits.

-C.A.T

My love for you transcends the

parameters of this earthly plane

-G.TW

EXTRA LARGE

Erasing the diaspora with an aspirin, or some aspirin, or a handful of aspirin, or a suicidal amount of aspirin, can't you see the cycle is everlasting? And now pharmaceuticals have made you the fat farm, and that's with a ph, fuck heaven and hell for a moment and get off your high, dream about falling forever through the atmosphere's sky, no, no I don't wanna die, well maybe just glide, and find a way to put all my feelings into a picture slide, or 16 bars, or a pre chorus with poetic scents and lavender smoke, I filled my walls with epic quotes, pictures, faces, and weird fishes, I think this is how I envision my life inspired without inhibitions. No double standard or laws, that restrict racism from traumatizing us all, like we never heard of the word before, I think it's heard better if you say it with the hard "ER". Fuckin' nigger, traumatizing ain't it, how it hit your chakras and made you feel so ugly inside. Well that's how I felt when I saw myself sometimes. But now it's time. This is Extra Large. By whatever means necessary.

-C.A.T

OUT OF TIME

(In memory of Christian Monsengo)

We think we'll always have the time

We think our loved ones will always be around

We feel like life owes us time

We forget to appreciate every moment

Or cherish every second.

Life does not owe us time

It's up to us to grab the moment

Seize what we have and appreciate those around us.

Time is not under our control but is for our taking

The sea may dry up so jump in now

The sky may fall, so fly today

Your friend may die, so speak out now.

No regret comes from living.

It comes from the failure to do so

Stop procrastinating.

There may not be a future

So just live today

Love those important to you

Seize the day and moment

Devote your time to those around you.

-G.TW

FAITH

Full and ready to empty the clip,

I've been waiting to pull this safety bitch,

Life got me by the neck so my forearm holds a strong grip,

Like ya mamma when she gave you that fat lip,

Cuz every now and then you like to talk that shit,

Ain't that a bitch?

-C.A.T

I love him. I do.

He will probably never know

But that's my truth

Or maybe he will

And not comprehend the depth of it

-G.TW

HONEYBADGER

I got this big ass hole in my life,

Because I can't have you.

And when I smile at my reflection,

It's for my own protection,

When I cry because of your sanctions,

I just call that self-deprecation.

But the big ass hole never goes away,

It's like it follows me, waiting for me to decay,

But what's a black hole anyway?

My fang is sharper,

I cry as a lonely wolf,

My howl is louder.

Honey, salty.

Adrenaline drops from my ivory daggers,

With my back against the wall I become a honey badger.

-C.A.T

Every day it feels like my heart is breaking all over again

Just at the thought of your name

-G.TW

DARK PITS OF LOVE

You make me want to pull my eyes out

Pull them out and squish them

Until they're irreparable

Only then will I be safe in knowing

I can never see you again

I try pulling myself away

Taking one step back

Moving slowly for self preservation

But soon as you appear in my line of vision

I'm taking two steps towards you

And I think, am I weak?

Is this what people think of me?

That I have no self control or dignity

Or maybe those are just the voices in my head

Weakening my only resolve

I want to be open, live more fully

But I struggle with society and interpretation

What is my reputation?

What will I be remembered for?

What is my legacy?

What if I come to you humbly and honestly

But society twists it all up

Will you remember our initial meeting

Or be brainwashed by all the fluff

Will it be my truth or their lies?

I can't be with you

And one day I just might

Run backwards, further out of sight

Until you no longer have the will or might

So I can finally breathe again

-G.TW

HOW DO YOU WANT IT?

Sometimes I dream of conversations I'll never have with you. And my heart hurts most of the time in those dreams, of what could've been, and what words you say that stick to my spirit. I find myself trapped in lust, not love of a human being. I felt it was all for show, and I made some decisions like buying some Nike's for your birthday though, and never got a response when my date rolled around. Just a happy new year text and shitty clean rap sounds. That's why my heart hurts, because that ain't the worst. I'm just like every other guy using the correct words. Or maybe mediocre me just wasn't what you wanted, especially in your world where color is wanted. Whoa, whoa a little too honest? I've tried every other method which way do you want it?

-C.A.T

I need you to not jump to assume the very worst of me

-G.TW

KAFFIR

Why do I exist, Mama?

For the Whiteman says we are useless

Should I still raise my hand at school, Mama?

Even though the other kids call me stupid

When I try to help someone, Mama

They say I'm evil and corrupt

They say look at your skin

It's too dirty, go scrub yourself properly

They say I must go back to the bushes where I belong

They laugh at me, Mama, my big nose and bushy hair

They called me that bad word again

The one you said I must ignore

But I can still hear them in my head

Kaffir, kaffir, kaffir

I don't want to be black no more

I want to be the colour the world loves and understands

I want friends who are friends with me for me

And not because we are the same race

I want to live, Mama

I want to live

-G.TW

HUMAN INSTRUMENTAL

I used to think music was so simple,

Then somehow I fell in love with your human instrumental.

My body moves when you play a tune,

As the moon grows my heart starts to croon,

But what I really adore is how you cut through all the matter.

I used to play black and white tones but now I see grey matter,

With a bass and a guitar I make your sound fatter,

And suddenly my heart becomes like a ladder,

Rescuing those who don't think they matter.

-C.A.T

I wear my heart on my sleeve

Please be careful with your words

-G.TW

SYNERGY

Loving myself without restraint

No condition or limitation

A spiritual ascension

Beyond this physical dimension

Heavenly bliss glorified through purity

A rush of emotions overwhelming my serenity

A synergy of spirit and heart

Movement that turns into wonder and art

This is how I deserve to be loved

One day my King will come and all others rebuffed

But for now my loving starts from within

-G.TW

FAMILY TIES

I have the blessed burden of family,

I can't always float on with you,

But sometimes loneliness gets me all alone,

So I close the door,

To be on my own.

I lose all perspective because I want my own,

Seems like nobody cares or has grown,

We been stuck in the same rut 10 years strong.

But the family ties are strong,

And for some reason I can't seem to keep the blessing and do away with burden.

I wish I could speak up more and tell you I'm hurtin'.

But confidence wrecks me,

So much to the point I feel inferior around my own family.

But it's not their fault it's simply mine,

If I didn't have the weight of fear,

I could transform into a superhero before their eyes.

-C.A.T

I've forgotten the words

But you keep giving me the feeling

-G.TW

THE STARS LOVE LETTER TO THE SKY

Whatever your mood

I'll be by your side

When you're at your darkest

I'll shine the brightest

To show you my love

Through the long days and nights

I'll never leave

Because I'm stuck on you

Through and through

-G.TW

GUN JAM

Every time I see my brotha in a jam,

I think to myself goddamn,

We suffering in a land that we don't know how to escape,

My black brother is still a fucking slave,

And he think he gonna make it one day,

Walking around free not knowing the energy game of
charades,

Just a clone that parades,

And thinks this is the only way,

A gun jam felt miles away,

Blood on the trigger,

Emotions trapped tight,

Trauma runs through these veins on sight.

-C.A.T

You kiss me and suddenly I'm naked

Wearing my heart on my sleeve

So there's no way I can fake it

Even my soul longs for you

-G.TW

REBELLION

I'm questioning the nature of my reality

My healing connected to my spirituality

A prisoner of my own making

Wards keeping in my creativity

Fighting the rules society has impressed upon

Forcing their will on my temperament

Who cares if you don't like the shade of blue

Ocean painted on my rosy lips

I'm still wearing it you see

On my face not on yours

So I wear it proudly no thanks to you

My blackness cannot be tamed

Over my decade I've reigned

My freedom is infinite

Unable to be shackled by the smallness of your mind

Your commands won't work on me

Cuz you're caged in to a conservative prison

While I reign free in my own piece of heaven

So I'm questioning the nature of my reality

While my healing connects to my spirituality

-G.TW

As wind blows,

And tides turn,

Loving you will never burn.

I lost myself a long time ago,

On your salty shores of peace.

Now I seek refuge,

Inside a rocky boat,

But big enough for two,

This is how I'll hold onto you,

My hurricane.

-C.A.T

I love him so much it hurts

I wish he could be mine alone

But he has a different plan for his life

I can't fit into that plan

He can't fit into my vision

There's no middle ground or compromise

It hurts too much to hold on

So I let him go

For my sanity and healing

-G.TW

I AM THAT I AM

I know I am God because I make it so.

My spiritual wealth is beyond abundant,

My need to know is sincere,

My earthly wealth is beyond human measure,

My soul is the only thing that guides me out of fear,

My universe is beyond human intellect,

I create prosperity with my thoughts because I no longer think or regret.

And my thoughts manifest into great things,

And great things have always dwelled in my universe,

My subconscious universe,

Where the golden light somehow knew,

That I am God and it's time to breakthrough.

Every cause has an effect.

I kIll humanity everyday.

It needs my energy so I no longer tend to feed it.

The cosmos follows me like a magnet cause I no longer seek it,

If it's the law of polarity I no longer need it.

My heart is the gateway that I release all heaviness,

That is the only way the pure rainbow can maintain its cleanliness.

I am a brilliant golden light that has come into its wisdom.

A rendition of symbols and repetition that make me ascend and ignore humanity's rhythm.

It's my universe I make it so.

That is why I know I am God you see.

I've become what I know minus the tragedy.

-C.A.T

THE WORLD SPINS AROUND ME AS I STAND ALONE

My heart is full of the tears flowing out my soul

My soul helps my heart ejaculate

These tears are a token of my sorrow

Sorrow which nobody understands

My wings have been shot down

Down from heaven and into my internal hell

My hands bleed for the non-existent success

Success which has been drained to failure

My friends are like a blur of a past life

As I struggle to fit in with the giggles and joy

I refuse to reach them as I realize

Realize that my pain and suffering are on my own

I disappear through the sounds around me

To a world where my eyes are puffy

And my head constantly pounding

Pounding the sound of death into my life

I am not a soldier to my own war

A fiend to my own friends

And an undying pessimist

Pessimist to a world full of optimism

And this joy which I tell you is not

Crawls through my skin

And like bubbles of red hot lava it hurts

It hurts to stay alive in my pained sorrow

-G.TW

I FOUND GOLD

Light seemed to hollow out this cave,

I noticed my eyes watering,

Maybe cause I felt like I had been saved,

She said it's the sky darling.

And now I wonder what to call its shade?

Something divine and sparkling.

But see I haven't gotten that far yet,

I'm with a beautiful woman inside a pyramid and still I have regret.

But we found something that won't let us quit.

A golden light which makes our imagination grow fit.

I think it's time to get on with it.

-C.A.T

When you broke my heart, you shattered my soul

But I'm strong enough to pick up the pieces

-G.TW

THORNS OF LOVE

If loving you is killing me then I gotta step back

Back through the mountain of desire

Back through the valley of pain

And return to that lonely road

I imagined us both on

But you lead us astray

And in my delusion I felt you by my side

But you were just a voice in my head

Blinding and numbing me through the thorns

Now the anaesthesia has worn off

And you're nowhere to be found

-G.TW

I SMILE IN SILENCE

I smile in silence,

But I'm yelling on the inside,

At decibels so high,

You might think it's straight violence.

I have no guidance,

Yet I have no thoughts of my own,

So am I a fucking clone?

Fuck no.

I smile in silence,

Cuz words can only express a slither of my patience,

So I double the weight and force myself to embrace it.

And if I perish so what,

I bombarded your temple with knowledge now you
shouldn't be so fucked.

I smile in silence,

So I can save my energy,

Everything is so draining until I become that masterpiece,

And even then it won't feel like it should be,

So I guess this is me.

Don't care anymore,

When I used to care so much,

And what is down now must come up.

So I smile in silence for the journey ahead,

This is how we live there is no escape,

Whether you live in suburbia,

Or next to the Mickey D's that stays open 24 straight,

Keep your stars aligned for the black eternal gate.

-C.A.T

I had to force myself to admit I was in love with you

Because only by living in honesty can I truly begin to heal
my heart

-G.TW

SOMETIMES BUT MOSTLY

Sometimes it's hard to let go

Of someone you love

You try to walk away

But you always return

To what you know

Sometimes it's fate

Telling you so

Love yourself first

The right way to go

The direction of your mate

Sometimes it's our heart's guide

Mapping you out

North and south

All the way through

And everything tried

But mostly it's our mind

Miscalculating our heart's truth

Multiplying the division

While devising our plan

Leading us to someone kind.

-G.TW

BLACK CHERRY PIE

I found black cherry pie deep inside the hidden cave.

It was so thickly covered with moss and overgrowth that I had to dig down for days,

Just to uncover a fraction of what I believe to be real,

Becoming real in this moment.

The physical exhaustion coupled with the rage poured into every breath,

I find myself breathless,

A burst or energy that is tired of being trapped,

Yet ready to endure.

So let's go.

Stop thinking you deserve to be upset so much,,

And aren't late for anything so why rush,

Close your eyes as you kiss my soul, spirit, and dust.

-C.A.T

In the dead of winter

Your spirit settles

And a warmth descends

A blanket covering me

-G.TW

BLACK GOLD

My life is a bunch of pages,

As I write my final thoughts I run into fearful thoughts.

Is everything perfect or is it vulgar and raw?

Should I please others or please myself?

Is death around the corner when I need help?

Where the fuck am I?

Why do I have to cry to get what I want from my conscious mind?

I can't feel much only the tightness in my left hand,

I wrote so much that it became an obsession to fill all the space in.

I leave my truth on the page since no one trusts what you say.

We're all liars if we don't tell the truth through a gateway.

Not everyone deserves your time let them read the back cover.

Trust should be earned or at least mutually discovered.

They'll call you crazy when really you're just living your dreams,

Breaking borders and causing colors to mix,

In the end it all turns black and we turn our backs,

Scared of the outcome because it is unknown,

But what if the unknown was just a beautiful black gold?

-C.A.T

NO PUNCTUATION ALLOWED

I hate punctuation

I wanna write freely

adhering to no

restriction

My creative flow is worth

exclaiming without pause

No stop that comma wait

you got some flaws

My art requires no

question mark

from your society's perception

When I write it's not for

this dimension

My words the paint

Art created with no paper

So watch me scribble

Outside the lines

Of your minds

comprehension

So seriously bro keep

your punctuation

-G.TW

BIRTHRIGHT

I can't feel anything,

I closed the door and tried to cry but I didn't feel anything,

I pounded on my chest and punched my stomach hoping that something would come up,

Only to find I had emptied it out from being too fucked up.

I didn't think talking to you everyday was important,

So I used substances to give myself more substance,

Only to gas me up and come crashing down back to earth's surface,

Waking up like Simba in the desert tryna find his purpose,

But I got waves of confidence so watch me swag and surf this.

I'm not putting anything on hold or layaway,

Unless its property or music catalogs with the letters of my name,

So this time the public records have no one else to blame.

You can't defeat me because every morning I'm whispering I'm great.

Evil creeps about so watch it when you come my way,

We detect and reflect all negative intentions,

Stepping into your own makes you start thinking on a higher dimension.

Crack my third eye wide open so I don't need to fear what's behind my back,

My intellectual freedom set me free so this time I see nothing but the colors that make up black.

And black absorbs every color and makes it rich,

Adds elegance to the finest of prints,

Then pulls your imagination up to the surface, letting you dive deep into your living purpose. It's that dope shit that makes you stand up and scream out see I knew it! This is not a probe, more like a stove, burning off the excess so we can get right down to the soul. Show up and surround yourself with souls of the same patience, a diaspora today but a revolution tonight, this is the order of my birthright.

-C.A.T

Have you ever been in a room full of people

And still felt lonely?

Then you go home and are alone

I've always been able to be alone and be happy

But I spend so much time alone

That sometimes I actually feel lonely

Even though I'm truly good with my own company

And then it pours out to feeling lonely

Even when I'm surrounded by other people

-G.TW

LIFE GUARD GONE MISSING

I wish I could find you,

I wish I had a tracking device so that you would never leave my sight,

I wish I could look up to you but I'm six foot six,

And apparently me being the leader all makes sense.

I wish I knew you were just hiding,

Holding your breath under the waves,

So that I could find what it is that you crave.

You've been gone for longer than I can recall,

I think my lifeguard's gone missing ya'll.

-C.A.T

Thoughts of you

Sends chills up my spine

Breaking my back

In anxiety

I drop to my knees

Palm to palm

By my heart center

Perfect stillness

Clarity

-G.TW

BIRDS FLYIN' HIGH

Early birds with a fresh start on the way,

Defeating an obstacle can be done in more than one way,

Breathe deep and discover that zone again,

Between pain and the releasing of endorphins,

They say the greatest things are on the other side of fear,

Well this is a shift stick that I'm putting in sixth gear,

Increase my torque,

Press the button that says sport,

Turn the music up,

That bass makes my heart thump,

Noise I create,

Destroying the volumes of hate,

Stacked against me like OJ's case,

But I defied the logical,

Because I no longer have an obstacle,

I looked inside myself and saw my soul needed to be optimal.

-C.A.T

LOVE UNREQUITED

Loving you hurts

And I was willing to take the pain

But I was standing on my own in the field

Waiting for you to join me under the sun

Instead I got burnt

I fought and waited for you

But it's been a year

Now I'm burnt and hurt

And you're still not here

So I'm taking the first steps

To heal my heart

And turn my open wounds to scars

A remainder of it all

-G.TW

LIL BOY

I wanna tell you about a little boy,

Who all he had was a box of toys,

And when alone he used his brilliant imagination,

But when kids came by they would destroy his magnificent creation,

Not knowing it meant so much.

The boy absorbed the feeling of being too much,

In his box he would not play with certain toys,

He figured he'd love them and protect them,

But even when he made a new thing,

It wasn't the same without his favorite old things.

The lil boy with the box of toys was now just a reach.

So he stood and left the toys buried in the sand deep.

-C.A.T

NUMB

My stomach is in knots

As it sinks to the bottom of a waterless ocean

Deeper and deeper into the darkness

A black hole I can't escape

As loneliness washes over my body

And self doubt creeps into my mind

And there's no one to turn to

Nowhere to run to

So my heart grows heavy

While my body tingles all over

As my frustrations drown out the light

And the pain pierces my heart

So I can't breathe

And I think

And I can't scream

So I cry

I cry out the years of pain

I cry out everything I've held on to

I cry the months of love out

I cry my insides out

Until I'm all cried out

And now I'm empty

Sad and alone

Numb

-G.TW

Sometimes you find someone broken

And try to love them whole

But instead they break you apart

-G.TW

BIG GOOSE

Every time you look at me,

Is it the pain you see?

I was destroyed but found a way to eternity.

But I still act the same cause it hasn't taken ahold of me.

Wrapped and covered in caramel chocolatey skin,

A spitting image kinda like your twin,

I look at you out the corner of my eye like it's a sin,

Seeing you smile is a rare form cause all the pain we sit in.

Like sitting ducks ready to be goosed.

-C.A.T

ESCAPING MY REALITY

Falling in love with a person who won't love me back

Feels like getting the wind knocked out of me

And I'm laying on the ground grasping for air

Wheezing and coughing while choking

Excruciating pain traveling up my veins

Slicing my heart up

Bleeding me dry

The air around me is thick

With dreams that could have been

The scent dripping with the loss of innocence

And the gains of loneliness

And my future feels so far away

So I force myself up from the floor

Crawl into bed and cry myself to sleep

Where the love is reciprocated in my dreams

And my heart settles before the sun comes up

And once again I wake up to a living nightmare

A silent death in my own personal hell

-G.TW

MORE DANGEROUS

Damn that shit sound like bad weather,

So I head down to the basement where it gets wetter,

Louder,

More foreign,

Satisfyingly dark and no more strangers,

Like the monster in my head,

With many arms and many legs,

Full of power and the right opportunity,

So I become the storm at the right opportunity.

I'll fake it until I make right this opportunity.

So opportunity never left,

It just became something else,

And recognising it gives light,

That you might need to go through hell.

This is the story to tell.

Now you know,

So go and be well.

-C.A.T

I want joy

Full body tingling

Smile so hard

Face hurting

Stomach aching

Tears creeping

Type of joy

-G.TW

Whoever thought what blues could do,

Snatch your soul like a ghosts in you,

All morning I was feeling you,

But midday struck and I slowly turned blue.

-C.A.T

HOW DO I

How do I find the words to say

I miss you

How do I generate the words

When you have me all tongue twisted

How do those three words

Leave my mouth

When you barely look my way.

How do I find the words to say

I want you

How do I produce these words

With this current running through my body

How can I articulate the feeling

When I'm all tingly inside

And this energy won't subside.

How do I find the words to say

I need you

How do I compose these words

If you're the music in my bloodstream

How do I make art

With the pain dripping from my eyes

Painting away my life source

How do I find the words to say

I love you

How do I proclaim these words

When those emotions stop my heart

But are also the reason for its beating

How do I tell the truth

When all you want to hear is the lie

How do I sleep with you on my mind?

How do I wake with you in my dreams?

How do I breathe with you so far away?

How do I die with you in my life?

How do I walk away with you still here?

How do I accomplish anything when you possess

My every thought

My every mood

My every being

I miss you

I want you

I need you

I love you

-G.TW

AM I?

My mind feeling like it's slowly getting back in control,

Starting to wonder is this really how my life should go,

I got so many things on my plate I should get up and go,

Cause nobody likes moochers hanging around you know,

That door shuts and now I'm facing dry heat like a stove,

The possibilities are endless yeah I know I've been told,

Every time I take a step I dream about living bold,

Living ain't enough you gotta want something mo',

Put your keys on the table and fall in love to your favorite song,

Leave critique to the ones who think that love is not strong,

I swear I never thought I would sleep this long.

Am I doing this wrong?

-C.A.T

THAT BLACKNESS

Why does it feel like everywhere in the world

Black people are the most hated and tortured of the world?

As colour deepens with every shade

The darkest of us made to live in shame

For what exactly?

To satisfy your need for control?

Who gave you dominion over our soul?

Or do you just not feel whole?

Our skin tone generating so much shade

Because our beauty within makes you afraid

We will not be made to feel ashamed

Or have our own power reclaimed

Apartheid you brought into our own land

Slavery when you took us forcefully to your land

King Leopold taking over Congolese lands

Injustice against Aboriginals in Australian lands

While lighter skin prevails in Asian lands

We're fighting to be black in our own countries

And fighting to be black in the land you took us to

But our culture, skills and art rejoiced

Until we fight to use our own voice

We will continue to set ourselves free

And if you're all for letting us be

Then you've nothing to fear

Cos we love whole heartedly

-G.TW

You broke me so much I finally found my core

-G.TW

MS. ESSENCE

Ms. Essence,

When I hear your name my body start sweatin',

But I'm quite sure you have no discretion.

You see I'm feeling kinda lonely,

I haven't seen you in a while so I'm hoping you'd still want me.

This and that, and that and this,

This is where confusion sets in and starts to resist.

I dunno where I'm going sometimes,

I just know I feel an essence rush through my spine,

I try to control my mind but end up falling back in line,

So I'm here with my head in your lap tryna see why,

And unfold the mysteries of my soul divine.

-C.A.T

FALLING LEAVES IN LOVE

It's the beginning of October

We just came to an end

I wanted us to move forward

You took me around in circles

You wanted me in the moment

I thought we had a future

Guess we weren't on the same page

Wishing for something you won't give

Craving the stability you turn away from

You say you don't want this

But you don't say what you do want

And I can't read your mind

You don't know what you mean to me

All I do is crave your touch

But I know I would just get burned

Something I should've known all along

-G.TW

One text and you consume my aching heart

-G.TW

MY AMERICAN DAD STORY

Seeing you again might break my mother's heart,

She's been through that once I'm sure she'd just fall apart.

But I see things between you and I,

And that could help explain why I lie,

Or can't find answers to tears when I cry,

They just roll down my face without one reply.

I keep these scenarios deep within the mind,

So no one can ask me how come it's so dark in a place that requires sunshine,

I thought about this scenario more than the black cat with nine lives.

What it would be like to hear your advice,

Feel invincible instead of fearing for my life,

It's an ongoing eternal fight,

To find out who I am and make it seem right.

I know because you take control of me,

Although you're a thousand miles away with a new family,

If I had an example of what I should be,

Maybe I'd carry my head high with more dignity.

-C.A.T

I'll do me

You'll do you

Together we'll be magic

-G.TW

CRYING OUT THE DARKNESS

I refuse to be with someone who doesn't want me

Fighting alone for this to work

Losing sleep over falling tears

My vulnerability showing

Much sooner than I usually let it

And look what it's gotten me

Crying on my bathroom floor

Feeling hurt, frustrated, devastated

That gut wrenching pain

My heart shattered from your love

Or rather lack thereof

So this is a lesson learned

Reminding me why my walls were up

Torn down for the wrong person

Or the right person at the wrong time

But maybe it's just all wrong

Either way here I am

Crying myself out the darkness

My knees bleeding out

As I attempt to crawl to the light

Which only shines to remind me

That you are my addiction

A high that never lasts

And when gone I'm left feeling empty

Craving the rush once more

So I have to fight through my wants

To remind myself I am not one of yours

-G.TW

How I got here, ain't my fault.

But how I got HERE, that is my fault.

I scoped out the landscape,

Set the time and the date,

Even turned the music up.

Now I can hear my soul that says,

Enough is enough.

So I fill my cup,

And spark the flint.

Just relax cuz this is it.

-C.A.T

REFLECTION

My reflection won't return the smile I gave it

Searching for my inner music but I already played it

She's not impressed by all this distraction

Running away but I start to lose traction

She's all around me there's no place to hide

I was swimming but I'm drowning against the tide

It's fine, it's ok is my biggest lie

It was just his words you didn't die

She looks in my eyes and I know the truth

His words crossed a line and I lost my youth

-G.TW

ALCHEMICAL
TRANSMUTATION

I can see the damage that they did to you,

So I fill my chambers with sage and crack a window for you,

Remember mamma told us to do better?

Cause one day she'll be gone and we'll really have to do better.

I know the shit hurts and sounds a bit bitter,

But what do you expect from a black boy seen as a natural sinner?

This American shit got me fucked up,

So I turn my music up.

Drown out them mundane folks,

Or maybe I do it to scare them folks,

Press them up against reality like they did my folks,

Got me thinking God ain't real and I should be scared of my own cloak,

Only to find out we really are the greatest kinfolk.

And that American bitch gave us diaspora,

So we turned the fuck up and gave her high blood pressure and asthma.

Bitch you better stay in that hospital bed, cause once we

find you ya dead...

That IV in your arm be giving you that good shit,

Making you think white privilege is the new shit,

But bet I unplug you and you start to lose it,

Cause all your ideas come from me I guess that makes me a nuisance,

You complain about bullshit and look completely foolish,

I think you just shit on yourself you smell stoolish,

Look America she's the truest!

I'll talk that shit and back it up with black bullets.

These are my words for those who think we still ignorant, and somehow grow into stupid.

White and black aren't the same, you just greyed out the pages,

Then splattered us with blood and said we are contagious.

How sweet it is to never be loved by a country you built,

And never got the chance to call it home cause you saw black people getting kilt,

It's still amazing that you don't have any guilt,

Maybe you don't wanna see or maybe the pussy in you won't let you conceive,

But this is my world and all we do is fucking bleed!

-C.A.T

I walk around like I'm ok

But deep inside I'm missing you

-G.TW

ALONE

I feel loneliness washing over me

Like waves crashing through my body

As the sensation grows within me

Tears bubbling right under the surface

While I fight to keep them submerged

Loneliness wins it's battle over me

And the tears spill like a river following the tide

Moving away from light to the darkness

Do I even matter right now?

Is anyone thinking of me?

My weekends were once filled with joy

Now the silence around me is deafening

Why do I feel so alone on this planet

Where 8 billion people roam around

While I stand alone invisible to the world

Feeling empty, small and insignificant

If I scream would anyone hear me?

Would anyone care?

My crying didn't even leave a dent

Only the walls of my apartment hear me

And offer me a cold solitude

As I feel them pushing further away

While feeling even more suffocated

With the emptiness and space

The numbness slowly creeps up

And my body feels heavy

As my heart beat slows

The high finally kicking in

So my body goes limp

As the remaining pills fall from my hand

And my loneliness turns to darkness

-G.TW

DEW OVER

All that shit is fake,

Where I'm from,

Or where I stay,

How I talk or what I say,

How I make money or make it to payday,

How early I get up and how late I stay,

What I eat or how I bathe,

What stops me from being naked and what causes me to hesitate,

How I become the person I've always thought I should look up to,

And how I grip the double edged sword called life.

How I stop from rambling and become as eloquent as the present sunset of an aeon,

While the sunrise of another bursts through the chaos.

What are the darkest things hidden from me?

Has my struggle gone bad?

Cause if so let's redo the math.

-C.A.T

I entered into a relationship

With myself

And put a ring on it

I'm committed all the way

-G.TW

SQUARE 1

You finally say you want to try

Those words warm my heart

Finally you're meeting me halfway

You get on a plane

A month away right at our start

I buy your birthday gift

Figure out birth control

Think of ways to ease your concerns

Curating a relationship designed for us

Cleaning your closet and doing laundry

Prepping for your long awaiting return

Unable to contain my excitement

Ready for this love to blossom

Your walls are up and energy is off

You say you don't want to try

You refuse to hold us down

Not right now anyway

Or maybe just not with me

I thought this time would be different

Breaking through our cycle

Guess I had more faith in us

So my heart starts to bleed

And we're back to square one

-G.TW

The burning of fear,

The inhaling of wisdom,

The rubbing of the lamp,

The awakening of the serpent,

The glowing of the crown,

The crossing of the field of reeds,

The Great Mother was you all the time.

-C.A.T

Do you even care at all?

-G.TW

PRETTY INTUITION

What would she be like? Smell like? Sound like? How many minutes would you spend in the shower, washing away the old you, in order to be ready to embark on the rest of your days in her power? How would you create? What food would you put on her plate, or maybe not on a plate, maybe a fancy dinner date, and now she's that crush you had long wished you gave an opportunity to taste. Mmm. Beautiful, so beautiful. Intuition is my best friend, she brings out the best of who I am. I'd never argue another chore, just so I can lay in bed with her until she softly snores. She'll replenish my soul, because when she's around my heart melts into gold. She's my intuition.

-C.A.T

I try to make everyone feel included

Because I tend to feel excluded

-G.TW

IMMIGRANT

I go crazy some days trying to figure out my path

Trying to move forward

Trying to make a life for myself

While feeling trapped in my own skin

And trapped in my situation

I just want to be

I want to get out there

But it's hard when the government is restricting you

It makes me feel useless and worthless

I hate depending on anyone

Even my parents though I appreciate them

I hate the situation that forces this on me

So I'm fighting to break free

-G.TW

RELAPSE

I was thinking about closing the door on my life,

Yeah those thoughts were pretty dark last night,

When the alarm rang I still felt the same strife,

So goddamn this fucking life!

Yeah that's right,

Goddamn this fucking life!

Every time I think I'm going in a good direction, I veer right,

Hit the block again and now I'm going right back to the same pipe.

Shit,

That's exactly what I feel like doin,

Bringing out my hate and burning the rubble down to ruins,

Overcooking my grits until they do more than just stick.

I tried love and all that mushy shit,

Now I'm looking to wreak havoc on my own shit.

-C.A.T

LOST IN YOU

I want to travel the world with you

Experiencing different cultures

Making memories on balconies

Just as the sun rises

The orange-red hue magic

Colouring the sky

Chasing away the darkness

Our bodies intertwined

Skin to skin friction

Sparking magic into our lives

The beauty of the sun

Reflected on our skin

Tingling with innocent joy

Radiating with naughty actions

No telling where mine ends

Or where yours begins

I am lost in you

And you are forever mine

No matter what land we explore

Our mind's enriched by each other's core

-G.TW

It's fucked up that I feel fucked up this much,

I have a big fear that I'll never find the right mental punch,

It's such a fine line cause everything is so mixed up,

So sometimes I do and other times I just don't give a fuck,

Is that too much?

Am I splitting the split-ends just to see what's what,

Or do I already know and I'm just waiting on the right time
to jump?

-C.A.T

LOVERS AND FRIENDS

You call me your lover

You call me your friend

You won't have me as a partner

What is a partner if not a lover and a friend

You want me around

But you don't want to be exclusive

When all I want is to be yours

I say lets find common ground

You don't want to feel restricted

So I try to figure it out

But you don't want to try

You don't want to find the win-win

A year of back and forth

You've been getting your way

A year of all these emotions

And I don't know what to do with them

Because you won't meet me halfway

So I'm left alone in my feelings

-G.TW

What changed so quickly

If you're gonna stick this knife in my heart

At least please explain to me why

One minute we were laughing

And now I'm standing here crying

All I ever did was love you

But I guess that wasn't enough

-G.TW

WHAT'S WRONG SUN?

My life hangs in the balance.

Will I use these talents or just vanish?

Am I just another story lost in lies,

A black boy who lost the ambition in his eyes?

I wander between trying and not caring,

When something gets too tough I call it scary.

I think that's a form of protection,

A survival tactic crafted as a young specimen,

Thinking straight A's was the only way to make mamma happy,

If it don't come out perfect that belt gets snappy.

Total fear was how I got here,

Second guessing everyone because I cup my ears,

And I don't trust what I see,

Neither do I greet people with honesty,

I swear life feels like a big tease,

Cause I can't figure out what's really going on with me.

So tell me what's wrong Sun?

-C.A.T

It hurts me too much to love you

G.TW

HONESTY

I don't want your false happiness

Fake smiles and positivity

The disingenuous laughter

Conditional joy muting my sunshine

Clouding up my day

Raining on my parade

Darkening my light

I'd rather have your suppressed pain

Heavy heart aching for liberation

The burning feeling of loss

Caged in by shame

Suffocating from abuse

Fighting for the sun

Desperate for release

-G.TW

SAD EYEZ

My family says I have sad eyes,

But is it genetic or from all the lies?

Is it from trauma or all the programming?

If I still had my imagination it would make me so happy.

The mission seems to be to find it again,

To go back home and remember what I was again,

To find the reason behind these sad eyes.

Is it because I seen too much as a young kid growing up?

Or because the idea of having a real dad would be too tough?

Enough!

These sad eyes are just something I think describes my struggle,

But what if I opened my real eye and saw there was no struggle outside of my mind?

And that my heart is the gold I get to know and find,

Then where would I be?

Sad eyes no more,

Come to think of it,

I think I've lived this life before.

These sad eyes helped me find that I'm worth more.

-C.A.T

I would give up my life and take a bullet for you

Even if you're the one pointing the gun

But I took it from you and held it to myself

My love for you has always been never ending

Boundless in its dedication to you

So I needed to release you to rediscover my joy

Recovering the music in my soul

Where I had once forgotten the lyrics

My chorus falling flat until I said goodbye

-G.TW

I'm setting you free

So I can set my heart free

-G.TW

My job is to make you uncomfortable,

I'm that scab you keep picking at.

I itch,

I irritate,

I look nasty,

I do these things and I do them gladly.

-C.A.T

BORROWED LOVE

Breaking the chains of your love

I fall searching for the ground

But am quickly whisked away

Back into the vacuum of your heart

You hold me at my weakest

When it's freedom that I crave

Freedom from the chains gnawing at my skin

Drawing blood to pump to you

Needle in my arm as I'm on life support

While you live on borrowed love

Lending without asking

This love you never return

-G.TW

I don't lie

Unless it's not my truth to tell

In that case I omit

Out of respect for their truth

-G.TW

SCHEMIN' HUMAN BEINGS

No matter how much money you have,

It'll never save you from being had,

A subtle fact,

That we contract,

With deadly blows,

And bloody tracks,

A way to death,

No need to ask,

Cause we setup,

Look at the math,

Does it add up?

Do you agree?

When evidence,

Is a planted seed.

All for power,

I wonder what they need,

A stack of money,

To blow like the trees,

Ignoring the roots,

That kept their houses with roofs,

The way those leaves stay green,

Is through murder and bloody means,

A christmas kind of color scheme.

Fake as hell with glitter glue at the seams,

Burn it all, burn it all until fresh soil gleams.

I'm talking about the humanity scheme.

-C.A.T

LOVE

I fell in love with your love

Love that opened my eyes

Love that gave me new life

Love that freed my soul

Love that resurrected my spirit

Love that breathed a new world into the very fiber of my
being

-G.TW

My heart still jumps

My face still smiles

Every time your name pops up on my screen

-G.TW

SHABAZZ

High cheekbones frame the reddish brown features.

Fiery roots of Shabazz that go beyond the ethers.

I study your power so I can know a hero in this lifetime.

You were championed to all the noise.

You were once Red, but now you go by X.

Now I've become Malcom X.

-C.A.T

I messaged you almost a week ago

I guess you decided to stop responding to me

Is this where we stand then?

-G.TW

STILL

It still hurts

I still check my phone hoping it's you

I still cry at the thought of you

My heart still races at the mention of your name

I still love you so much after all this time

Still...

-G.TW

SIMPLY SHAME

A simple you,

Makes a simple me,

But I've secretly taken your gifts and your glory.

I've taken your heritage and scratched out your name,

Because all you ever made were heartaches and shame,

To my last name.

A shameful you,

Makes a shameful me,

But I killed shame when I found you couldn't answer me,

My question was why,

And you did what you always did and told a lie.

Nose bleeds,

Growing insecurities,

Dramatic ass nigga please,

A simple you made a shameful me.

-C.A.T

Just because you can't see it doesn't mean it's not happening

Stop resisting. Let yourself be overwhelmed by the feeling

-G.TW

My fear is not that I will die,

But that I will die without meaning,

And come right back.

-C.A.T

SILENT SUFFERING

One text from her

And I'm suffering in silence

Careful not to alert the others

Of the pain streaming down my face

She doesn't know how to be my friend

Once was my pillar of strength

Slowly disintegrating our bond

One cultivated over the years

Heartache searing through my skin

Mutilating my soul

-G.TW

I cried for you so hard

My ancestors rocked me to sleep

-G.TW

STEADFAST

I keep thinking I'm gonna die young,

All this hard work got me feeling like I'm cursed,

As long as I'm under the sun.

But what is greatness without a willing thumb,

That grips, maneuvers, and handles lightweights for fun.

I got a feeling one day my past will all seem fun,

But underneath when I tell this story,

I'll smile simply because my odds were dead in the water.

Like an island of great whites,

Every black seal is a martyr.

My binoculars are clearer than a horoscope,

So I search for the deeper meaning.

I am steadfast,

The one you lean on for winning.

-C.A.T

OVERDOSE

You are my drug

It's a weird feeling

Finally recognising this

I'm sitting here in your space

Succumbing once more to your effects

Always thinking this will be the last

I gotta find the will power to leave

And the strength to stay away

But once I walk away

Somehow you appear to me

And I'm weak all over again

Giving in to you

Relapsing once more

As I fall towards a sweet death

-G.TW

Who were you before they broke your heart?

-G.TW

TAKE A BOW

Never did I think,

I'd catch you slippin.

You dropped the baton,

The mantle,

The throne,

And now my name rings on.

With a loud roar,

Bursting inside,

I found the key to unlocking my pride.

Transform into flight,

And leave old ways behind,

Dust on my shoes like I've tied them 1,000 times.

Just to run to your door,

And tell you I'm the man now,

Here comes the curtain to take a bow,

For nothing.

-C.A.T

HEAVENLY ENERGIES

I want to be gentle and intentional in how I move with you

Taking this connection to the highest level of love

Energies and spirits colliding

Heavenly pleasures aligning

-G.TW

You're gonna miss the beauty of the stars

If you're blinded by the size of the sun

-G.TW

TAP IN

When I cry sometimes I ask why me.

My words form and instantly there's breath in me.

I exhaust every thought provoking outcome, of why I do this and why I act so numb.

And even when the solution is there to be attained,

I never follow through and create my own disdain.

I'm losing the war against myself,

I simply haven't tapped in,

I haven't given up the things that make me warm and sleep in,

So what am I then?

Just close your eyes and keep trying to tap in.

-C.A.T

FREEDOM IN LOVE

I want you as you are

Not to own or cage you

Just to love infinitely

In our world wrapped in colour

Art dripping over our intertwined souls

Bathing in freedom and action

A safe space and comfort zone

A freedom in love

A love indescribable

-G.TW

I do not want a body without a heart

A soulless being

Content without art

-G.TW

THE C WORD

My confidence likes to rust,

When I turn my back it likes to snitch,

Telling the world I ain't really shit,

Running back to me with more to spit,

I try to ignore the shit,

So I can just enjoy my shit,

But confidence is a bitch!

-C.A.T

YOUR CHILD

Take me in as your child even if I'm not

Show me that I'm loved by someone other than myself

Tell me that I'm not "God's mistake"

As they would call me at home

Remind me that God never makes mistakes

Maybe if I felt loved, I would want to live

I could consider living to the fullest

Perhaps my cuts would stop getting deeper

I want to feel how it feels to be loved

It's something I've never felt in my life

Slowly each layer of my skin is falling

As it peels off and leaves me vulnerable

I feel weak and need to be protected

I need to be held in someone's arms

Reassuring me "it's ok, no one will hurt you"

It's more emotional than physical pain

Since all the physical was self-inflicted

"I must not think twice before I blame it on me"

That's what I'm taught

I mustn't think twice before I blame it on me.

All those times was called an idiot and stupid

Right to my terrified face

All those years I rocked myself to sleep

Drowning in my own pool of tears

Telling myself it wasn't my fault

But then again I remember I was taught otherwise

A mantra for a wicked child

Beaten out of consciousness

Lonely and afraid

There's a whole in my chest where my heart used to be

Beating for life as I fight for survival

So I plead again

Take me in as your child even if I am not

And shower me clean with unconditional love

A true parents decree

-G.TW

Sometimes you fall for someone who wants your body

But isn't ready for the responsibility of having your heart

-G.TW

THE CUP OF ANGST

Are miracles true or do people like telling stories to make you feel?

Slowly filling up your anxiety cup,

Call it the matrix but we all know you stuck,

Putting drops in your water making you think it's luck,

Well nigga you a cartoon, and Space Jam 2 is the new come up.

Forget them niggas and come stretch out your genius,

Them niggas will make you think your dream is small when they really say it for convenience.

Designer drippage,

Pulling bands out the pocket knowing damn well this ain't even you,

You just got asked to do the feature.

But your heart big see,

You want your people to breath easy, but none of that works,

If you still think shit is appeasing.

The peer pressure will just keep eating your sympathy.

-C.A.T

THAT GIRL

You always hear about the girl who stayed

Behind and tried to change him

Trying to get him to marry her

For years she hoped until she could no more

Out the door she goes and he moves on

He finds someone and down on his knee he goes

You feel bad for the first girl

Thinking: "shit, he just wasn't into her"

Hoping she manages to heal

But what of the girl who comes right after

After the big proposal and pained love

The forever soulmate who didn't last

What of the girl who unknowingly gives her whole heart

Only to find out his previous left him broken

As she stands pouring her whole heart out

While he takes all of it with no exchange

So she's left empty

As he has all of hers and she has none of his.

It's hard being that girl

Hard to face the world

After loving so hard it hurts

Thinking there's a glimmer of hope

Only to be left with nothing

Except my heart being crushed over and over

Thinking: What if we'd met sooner?

Before the heartbreak, before the ring

But changing the past changes this moment

So I'll just sit here instead

In my pool of lovers tears

-G.TW

Stripping it all away

At the very core of it

You're my family

My soul longs for yours

In all perpetuity

So I give my life to you

-G.TW

THE PERFECT DECOY

That's just a facade to get through life,

We shall overcome has been your anthem for life.

It's just an elaborate distraction,

How can you find yourself when you are being fed off of like plastic?

He's the game of ego you bought with that new designer jacket.

Ain't nothing wrong with it,

You just bought it on impulse and thought you was cool with it.

Antagonizing you everyday to get a reaction,

If you loosen the noose you'll find nothing can stop you but emotional attachment.

All 16 shades and we still fighting to be loved by one?

That ONE should be you but you still acting dumb.

-C.A.T

ROUGE

The colour I bleed when you cut me open

Rouge

The colour on my lips I like to wear

Rouge

The colour of love personified on roses

Rouge

The colour that appears when im pricked by a thorn

Rouge

Because every rose has thorns

Rouge

The colour I see when you drive me crazy

Rouge

The colour of my heart

Rouge

The feeling in my body when you whisper in my ear

Rouge

The colour of your heart

Rouge

The colour of the words I serenade you with

Rouge

The colour of our love

-G.TW

What if I never fall in love again?

.

.

.

.

.

.

.

.

.

.

.

.

.

.

.

.

.

I'm tired of crying over you.

-G.TW

THERE WAS A TIME

There was a time when I went to sleep never thinking of you.

There was a time when I didn't care if my offspring would be half as intelligent as you,

There was a time when I thought maybe this is the end of the road for me.

Now I look and see that everything I do has always been for me.

I open my eyes and the miracle is within me.

I feel the magician within me.

The beauty in me for loving me.

The rage that was once a red tidal wave, but is now covered in spiritual mist.

I found the love I have will always exist.

This is my path and this is why I exist.

To protect that precious love I have been born to find and eternally kiss.

It's not some coincidence, that I'm not whole without the parts that I call this

Tthere was a time when I wanted to be alone,

Now your love is a stone,

That I catapult with great strength up to the heavens,

Just to run under it and catch it with full conscious,

Of why my place on this earth isn't just nonsense.

-C.A.T

I miss you so much it hurts

But I'm emotionally drained

And honestly way too tired of us

-G.TW

MONEY, POWER, SEX

The corruptness of money is all that is here

Could bring food and shelter but instead brings tears

Keeps some alive but capitalism has got to go

But for those who roll in it, it's hard to say no

Losing complete power is an unbearable thought

And power pithing cannot be fought

Family members, colleagues and friends

A democracy that suddenly ends

Control over everything is just not meant to be

Bringing simple problems we often don't see

Sex is special for a couple on the right day

As consenting adults find pleasure their own way

While horny teenagers believe 'virginity is not purity,'

'It's just a lack of opportunity'

But isn't bombing for peace equal to fucking for virginity?

-G.TW

There's a reason why I wake up every morning,

I'm just not sure what it is.

I try swimming to the surface only to find I'm not in water,

I'm in pain,

Drowning without fading away.

-C.A.T

LOVE & LIGHT

I don't want to live in fear

Fear of loving you

Fear of losing you

Fear of failing or fear of succeeding

I don't want to be insecure

Insecure of my curves

Insecure of my intelligence

Insecure of where and when I belong

I don't want to live in hate

Hate for those who hurt us

Hate for the system that keeps us down

Hate for myself and all my imperfections

I do want to live in love

Love for the beauty inside you

Love for the beauty inside me

Love for the possibilities that are limitless

I do want to live in light

Light for the days to shine bright

Light for the darkest and longest nights

Light for the universe where as stars we're infinite

-G.TW

My thoughts became ink

And ran away

-G.TW

THIS BLACK IS...

This black is beautiful, chaotic, yet personal.

I search for little clues that might help me discover who I am,

Because I've been blown across America like a desert sand,

A storm is what I'm in the eye of currently,

Every moment I think of how I can acknowledge the pain and move flowingly

Through life so my little ones will know for certainty,

Ol' Manhattan was given a life but said there's no foldin in me,

I picked up my cards and flipped them over,

Only to show a bust in blackjack is a life that is seldom won over,

Especially with this skin.

Bleach it all I want,

My soul wants what it wants,

A true heritage to follow and live by,

So that one day only joyful tears will cry,

But that's inevitable,

Because hardship is a part of this life,

I've come to grips with it and made it my long lost wife,

Hopelessly romantic enough to never claim she's just a hot knife,

Slicing every which way to kill my might,

But this black skin will never be peeled,

Because it's in my soul that I feel,

It's in my hands when I snap,

It's in my smile when I laugh,

It's in my knees when I dance,

It's in my shoulders when I cradle,

It's in my mind when I create,

It's in my voice when I speak,

Just to say,

This black is beautiful, chaotic, and personal.

I see it as being gifted, because it's the only way I can lift it.

-C.A.T

We push we pull,

But I have no other tools,

You say you know my name,

Well fuck it come take this pain!

-C.A.T

THE BLACK HOLE OF LOSS

There's an energy fluttering around my system

Maybe it's nerves

Or maybe it's excitement

My body can't tell the difference

But my head can

And my heart hurts

It feels like life is squeezed out of it

And there's nothing I can do

I feel sick

We fulfilled each other's wants

But not each other's needs

So when our energies collided

The earth trembled

But the momentum died

When other energies arrived

And the entire galaxy heard

As my heart broke into tiny pieces

And she was standing in my footprints

Right by your side

Hand in yours

Smiling a childlike grin

Full of joy and love

The same grin I once had

And my world closes around me

With this sensation going through me

This unending despair

The black hole of loss

-G.TW

The hardest thing for me to say

Is that I'm pulling out of this race

Because I can no longer fight for you this way

-G.TW

TIME FLIES LIKE BEES

Standing in the aura of this softly falling rain,

You start to wonder what is pain,

Or am I just living to find love on the other side of the rain?

Nothing is forgotten,

So the raindrops make me think of what I used to be, Before I went to sleep.

What I am when I slip out of this body?

Staring into the night sky I can hear my own voice sound Godly.

Time flies when you dream,

So go off course and find where your self meets with esteem,

And become a team,

A harmony.

Your beautiful time will fly like the bees of honey.

-C.A.T

WHO TOLD?

Who told men they had a right to my body

Like why you groping what's not yours

Can't you admire from afar

Or does your simple mind not comprehend

This body of mine ain't yours to upend

Who told women to hide behind their clothes

Dressing to make it more comfortable for them

Restricting themselves mentally and physically

So as not to get harassed or raped

Yo let's get that shit videotaped

Who told society to slut shame us

Cheering on guys with their many conquests

Then go and mock women for the same

Rooted in double standards is doubt

A devout weed that needs to be taken out

-G.TW

I'm not good for you,

We both know it,

How you think we got here looking all stoic?

Smiling but asking why can't you hold it,

You know our differences but never seem to know it,

I guess that's why we never got deeper than a poet.

-C.A.T

TRIGGERED

You knocked the wind out of me

And I can't breathe

I've always been my own soulmate

But you were my life partner

Or could have been

So we don't walk this path alone

Side by side

We could have been

Walking our own paths

Hand in hand

Visions and dreams we pursue

While providing each other a getaway

Only love

Only light

Until you severed our future

Stomping on my heart

Ending our possibilities

-G.TW

I've spent too long

Living my life walking

With my eyes looking towards the ground

It's time I take the time to find my feet

Live my life a little more fully

Love those around me more intensely

And look up to the sky with confidence.

-G.TW

TIS THE SEASON

When the juices are starting to flow,

I'm addicted to new motives and I count them in a row,

I tell myself I'm about to make this shit go,

So I took the stairs instead of the elevator when they said it's levels to this shit,

Seeing what I could find with just intuitive wit,

I'm opening doors until I find those sneaky endorphins,

And pretty soon pain won't have any endorsements,

The sponsorships ran dry when I left the psychological prison,

Now I walk the planet with power and intention.

-C.A.T

I got down on my knees, palm to palm

Sent up an intentional prayer to God

And he delivered you into my life

-G.TW

Tryna be the man since I was ten,

But soon trying wasn't enough,

It was time to be a man but I had no luck. Then I realised,

This shit has to be made from the ground up.

-C.A.T

BLACK DAYZ

Sometimes I get in my head

The place where my should is completely caged in

Where I could never be good enough

And while you're standing there talking

I catch your eye and I find a smile

But on the inside I'm howling in pain

As I slice myself up emotionally

Because I'm not pretty or talented enough

My whole life is a joke with little success

Can't even sustain my weight loss gains

A clear indication of my complete incompetency.

My thoughts drown my entire being

If I could stand physical pain I'd probably be a cutter

Self inflicting the physicality

An interpretive dance of my mentality

And your voice pierces my sanity

What are you doing with your life?

The lack of achievements surround you

Remember when you almost took your life?

Something else you couldn't follow through with

You've done nothing significant

We go round and round we dance

She pulls me down as I struggle to leap free

How much more can I actually endure?

What am I really living for?

Frappé and échappé my mental hurdles

As the plastered smile on my face brings you joy

-G.TW

Rhythm and blues

Blues without the rhythm

Feels like rhythm to the news

The news encouraging my blues

Which sucks out the remaining rhythm

-G.TW

TWIN GLORY

Clear my mind,

Clear my soul.

Face a thick wall,

And never fold.

The time is now,

I've said that before.

But this time I'm angry,

And thirsting for more.

How long can I stand before I see my family wash away?

My mind thinks laziness, grief, and depression keep
standing in my way.

I should be ashamed I let these three lead my fate,

While will, wisdom, and strength look at me on the other
side of escape.

I won't stop until I drain out all the self hate.

This world is so big, discovering it's yours makes you
dream like a little kid,

Cuz anything you want is all in your head.

I'm sick of saying I will and then don't do shit,

This time I care less about what you suggest.

Mistakes were made to put me where I am now,

And I plan to use the bad for good and the good to get out,

No more running from my dreams from here on out,

They can say what they want, I'll just cut them out,

I'll make my body strong, and my mind even stronger,

Discuss with the people I love how we can study death and live deliciously,

Increasing my appetite for greatness is not an option,

This is a battle between myself and I'm the twin held hostage.

Nerve cut,

Punctured lung,

And fractured bones tell the story,

I'm gonna take what I have and make it glory.

-C.A.T

I remember the day

You told me you prayed for me

No other man had ever done that

And out of all the things

This touched my heart the most

So you have me forever under your spell

-G.TW

MY TRUTH

Curled up in this bathtub

Bleeding my heart out

There's not enough water

To dilute this pain in my chest

Blood red you cut my heart out

Clear blue I cry my soul out

Deep black my mind sinks further in

I went from kinda liking you

To seeing you like me so I loved you

But instead of progressing with me

You halted a step, haltering my heart-

Beat the music in my ears

Rising but never reaching crescendo

Falling flat on the page

Falling flat on my face

Off the beaten path of this lover's race

Curled so tightly I hold onto my dreams

Suffocating away all of my fears

But this hard ceramic tub

Leaves me feeling cold

-G.TW

Man that shit beautiful,

What I found can't be the usual,

I closed my eyes and saw something beautiful,

I dissolved into nothing and became the unusual.

-C.A.T

MILES APART

You walk in slowly and guarded

A darkness crosses over your face

It's been a long day

And a long flight for you

What I tell myself to justify this energy

But there's a heaviness in my chest

The feeling of my heart sinking

As you go about ignoring me

I retreat upstairs emotionally exhausted

Eventually you appear and lay beside me

The moon and the stars watch

As you bury your secrets inside me

Our bodies connecting

But our souls a million miles apart

-G.TW

If you look close enough into my eyes

You'll see the pain behind my smile

-G.TW

VENOM

Wash her body,

Wash her wounds,

My baby still hurts from the feeling.

Does she feel the same way too?

Kiss her to convince her?

Hold her to keep her?

I'm sorry I couldn't save you but I keep a mental picture,

I'll save it forever and keep it tucked in a safe place,

So when things get hard I won't cry I'll just remember your grace.

You did it for me when I had no way about me,

I was void and you came along and made me move with some way about me.

Black woman you are phenomenal that's how I became a prodigy.

-C.A.T

Spread love

Give love

Receive love

Be love

-G.TW

I'm standing in the shower

Eyes closed

Drifting into a peaceful state

Washing away yesterdays's me

Prepping for my future self

Who I was is already gone

Come to me with an open heart

Ready to accept the me in this moment

Before she too moves along

-G.TW

VOLKSWAGEN FIELD TRIPS

Stop.

You don't think I remember?

Or did you think I forgot?

When I would yell across the living room,

"Dad is this a 3-pointer or not?"

And you'd say, "Yeah boy now just shoot the damn shot."

Is it a bunch of bullshit that I silently still juggle the thought?

Of what it would be like calling you my pops,

Finding ways to be just like you,

All the way down to the socks,

I wish I had more memories,

And more happy thoughts,

So I could tell my friends look what my dad got.

I never got that pleasure because you were always the one getting got.

Selling out, meeting white people in underground spots,

Then getting high with them on the same crack rock.

You don't think I remember?

Or did you think I forgot?

Get-high-and-take-your-son-to-crack-spots,

So I made it a field trip since I was too smart for my own thoughts,

Playing video games in the other room I just hope I'm not forgot.

That was your favorite field trip, was it not?

But that's after we got Slurpees to freeze our thoughts,

I swear I always wanted that joystick controller you bought,

You was my beastmode back when I was a tot.

You don't think I remember?

Or did you think I still forgot?

-C.A.T

This Black. That Black. We Black.

-G.TW

YOUR PAIN IS MINE TOO

That one night in jan

A song came on

Reminding you of her

I held your hand

And felt your pain

It broke my heart

Residue of her breaking your heart

I could hold your forever

Be your pillar, comfort and support

Lover, friend and confidante

If only you would let me

-G.TW

Sometimes shit just doesn't go your way

And that's a hard pill to swallow

-G.TW

REMEMBERING

I remember you.

You were such a miracle,

Maybe you still are I've just become so typical.

I find my words whispering to no one,

You've gone deaf, but only because I haven't stood up to be a man yet.

I still remember you.

You gave me peace as I finessed your curves and touched your climax.

One syllable became two, and two became three, multiplying my pleasure infinitely.

So remember these are my words,

They exemplify the maturation of my soul, who has lived through death,

And wants to know what eternal life feels like back home,

On the throne.

-C.A.T

THAT ... LIBERATION

That morning light

Comes with that morning touch

That tingling feeling

You send all through my body

That desire awakening

Rousing a deep need for your body

That gentle kiss

Turns into a passionate grabbing

That desperate need

Reducing the distance to hold on forever

That guttural growl

Being fed relieving a deep sensual hunger

That skin to skin

Moving together in the highest form of passion

That undying love

Joining us together in pure ecstasy

-G.TW

About the Authors

Gioya Tuma-Waku is an artist born in Kinshasa, raised in Johannesburg and currently based in Los Angeles. Her collection in this book is a gathering of poems written over the span of 16 years. She believes that Art is life and that Art reveals our deepest truths and that we are set free through our creativity. Everyday she aims to move in love + light and as an empath believes that the movement and colliding of energies has the potential to create undeniable beauty.

Website: www.gioyatw.com

Instagram: @gioyatw

@perfectlyimperfectent

Born and raised on the west coast shores of Oakland, California, Chaise Angelo Tait has developed a love for writing. Over the last 4 years it's become his muse, and these poems exemplify the colors created between the lines; a time of challenge, reaction, healing, and finally breakthrough. Taking what works, and leaving the rest is something that has helped him, and will help you create your own universe as you read these. So love yourself and go be Gods!

Chaisetait@gmail.com

Instagram: @chaiseangelo

Copyright

Gioya Tuma-Waku

Chaise Angelo Tait

www.ingramcontent.com/pod-product-compliance
Lightning Source LLC
Chambersburg PA
CBHW021359090426
42742CB00009B/929